BRONX MIGRATIONS

Bronx Migrations

poems by

MICHELLE M. TOKARCZYK

Cherry Castle Publishing

Cover photograph: "EL Line North of Tower Above 149th Street"
1974 by Jack E. Boucher

Cover Design: Deb Dulin
Edited by Truth Thomas & Melanie Henderson
Copy Editor: Susan Thornton Hobby
Author Photograph: © 2016 by Melanie Henderson

All rights reserved.
Published in the United States of America
First published as a Cherry Castle paperback 2016

ISBN-10: 0-692-73765-0
ISBN-13: 978-0-692-73765-1
#
Library of Congress Control Number: 2016944294

Cherry Castle Publishing, LLC
P. O. Box 6355
Columbia, MD 21045
www.cherrycastlepublishing.com
where words grow mighty trees

ACKNOWLEDGMENTS

Thanks to the following publications in which some of these poems first appeared:

"The Arson Years, 1970-1980," *NewPeople: Pittsburgh's Peace and Justice Newsletter*, (February 2014): 6.

"What He Said," *Slant* 28 (2014): 93.

"A Personal History of the Bronx River," "The South Bronx, 2011," and "Shopping at Alexander's Bargain Basement," *New York Dreaming*, (September 29, 2013), http://www.newyorkdreaming.net.

"Beacon, 2010" *The Leopard Seal*, Issue 1, (Winter 2013), https://youtu.be/2cZ_Ls3fZYI.

"On Tremont Avenue," "Woyko," and "Granny's Funeral," *Third Wednesday*, (Summer, 2012), http://www.thirdwednesday.org.

CONTENTS

ACKNOWLEDGMENTS   v

MISSIN' THE BRONX BLUES

The Stoop, Daly Ave, 1961	3
The Third-Grade Teacher at St. Thomas Aquinas, 1961	4
Jasmine	5
Shopping at Alexander's Bargain Basement	7
Walking the Bronx Apartment Hallway	9
Migration from West Farms, 1962	10
Crossing Over	11
Nights	13
Visiting the Bronx Zoo	14
She Sees an Addict	15
How to Walk in West Farms, 1964	16
I Made a Promise	17
On Tremont Avenue, 1961	18
Old Friends	19
Safety	20
Missin' the Bronx Blues	22

TRYING TO BREATHE

For the Girls: Mom Speaks	27
Trying to Breathe	29
Granny Moves to Kingsbridge Road	31
Woyko	32
Granny in the Nursing Home, 1976-1978	33
Granny Refuses the Amputation	35
Granny's Funeral	36
Waiting	37

LEARNING

Peacock Escapes from Bronx Zoo	43
Left Behind	45
Food Stamps Sonnet	47

Roaches	48
Memories of Orchard Beach	49
Riding a City Bus in July	51
Lehman College, 1970s: The Campus	52
Climbing the Steps of Carman Hall	53
Learning	54
What I Didn't Know about Hip Hop	56
The Co-Op City Resident after 9/11	58
A Summer Vacation	59

WHAT HE SAID

The Master Builder's Cross Bronx Expressway	65
The Arson Years, 1970-1980	66
What He Said	67
The Father	68
Presidents Visit Charlotte Street	70
Happy Land Fire	72
On Fort Apache, the Movie	74
Blackout	79
Mural for Amadou Diallo	81

TRICKSTER

The Nightmares End	87
In the Archives	89
The South Bronx, 2011	90
She's Teaching in Suburban Maryland	91
A Personal History of the Bronx River	93
Beacon, 2010	95
The First Shot	97
Jackson Heights, 2014	98
Poetry at the Bronx Museum	99
Elegy for a Building	101
Trickster	102

ABOUT THE AUTHOR   104

To the people who lived and live in the Bronx

Bronx Migrations

Missin' the Bronx Blues

The Stoop, Daly Ave, 1961

My mom, forehead threaded with worry,
stays inside. The chatter of TV characters
backstory to forming hamburger patties.

Downstairs I watch Mary Gubar's
out-of-place wooden house,
slumping in a block of low-rise apartments.

Its blue paint fades into summer, cats
(I'd heard) creep through holes,
but I've never seen one.

Next door the synagogue. Once
from Granny's window I saw a man
with the long beard and small cap on his head.

Was he carrying a book? I was afraid
to look too closely, to commit a sin
by observing another religion.

The candy store is just one block away.
When others come out to play
we cross one traffic light for penny treats.

Later we'll mark the block with a game of hopscotch
boxes chalked hard, lines clear.

Upstairs Donna Reed is trapped in TV.
Down here I'm on the stoop.

The Third-Grade Teacher at St. Thomas Aquinas, 1961

She needs a glass of Tang every day before class.
Bright orange powder stirred into water from the fountain.

The astronauts, we know, drink Tang.
So easy to store and loaded with nutrients,
it keeps them strong as they whirl in empty space.
Nothing holds them down, nothing to hold onto.

In twenty years how many students carve initials
into Miss Kennedy's desks? How many mark
their presence as she tries to mark their minds?
She doesn't always get their accents or their home lives
shoved somewhere in their frayed bags
                                     where homework should be.
She doesn't feel cold floors cracking splinters, walls chipping lead,
old blankets pulled tight against rats scraping through the night.

When their heads settle on their desks her lessons are a lullaby,
no pitch of argument or worry. What, she wonders, is her job?

Wake them gently.
They're weighted down but weightless,
Drifting, waiting to fall.

Jasmine

Our mothers walked us to school,
talked about teachers and tests.
We ran ahead, and I tried
to pace my steps to the strides
of Jasmine's almond legs, to match
the volume of her words. "Mom, why
can't I play outside today? Please!"

I watched her finger follow words in books,
her legs cross at her ankles, like mine.
And I wondered how anyone
could make Jasmine a slave. Or why anyone
would see Jasmine's dad and be afraid.

Mom told me Jasmine's family,
with their starched ironed clothes
and lists of chores, were *different* Negroes.
But I saw Jasmine's thick braids
that never bounced, the soft brown
color of her arm next to mine.
I knew they were no different.

A year later we hugged good-bye.
They moved to the North Bronx,
to a smaller apartment and a new school
where, I heard, Jasmine had no friends.
Afternoons she stayed at home. Read a lot.

A decade later on the Number 7 train
my family had the whole empty car.
Then, a young man boarded: Afro framing
his dark face, legs apart, claiming his seat.

Our parents grabbed our hands, ignored
our "whys," walked us through
the jolts of the moving cars.

And I knew we were no different.

Shopping at Alexander's Bargain Basement

On Fordham Road off the Concourse
that used to be so grand,

women scavenge the tables.
Chapped reddened hands
and circled eyes search

for the jacket like Jackie wore,
the green-checked shirtwaist
with a slight imperfection.

Be quick, or someone else
will grab that find. Take the chance.
No return on final sales and who

has time or stomach to strip
in the dressing room, flimsy
curtains revealing cellulite.

Dad, running errands for Granny,
loved a bargain, had to stop,
took his chances, found

the bin of girls' shoes. Clearance.
Less than a buck apiece.
He bought a dozen pairs,

more or less our size, some
real leather. Came home
just as Nan and I were going to bed.

Mom let us stay up, watch him pull out
pair after pair. He'd hold the soles
in his hands, twist red oxfords,

penniless loafers, before we tried them on.
Our feet filling them out, we saw ourselves
walking proud.

Walking the Bronx Apartment Hallway

As a cat rubs its body across your leg,
I stroked my fingers along the circular
swirls of plaster, traced the sizes of bumps
in the ridges, let the walls' coolness soothe my hands.

I think of those walls engulfed by flames
or smashed by wrecking balls.
And I hope some of the surface
permeated my fingers, radiated up my arms.

When I rented my own apartment
even my poor student friends gulped.
Ground-floor windows faced an air shaft
and never saw light.
Soot filled the panes' deep cracks.

But the walls' plaster swirls captivated me.
Their contours held the texture of home.

Migration from West Farms, 1962

Her last day before the move that
her parents thought they must make,
but would always regret,
Miss Kennedy called her to the desk,
looked straight at her bent head
and said, "The nice ones always go."
It should have been a good day,
but she missed the teacher's question
on national resources. Her last question.

Lunch hour, the other girls chat and giggle
around her like she is already gone.
Peanut butter and milk swallowed down,
she files outside. The schoolyard,
never built, long ago forgotten.
Children spill onto the sidewalk,
into the street now closed to traffic.

Shoulders hunched, hands stuffed
into her coat pockets, she sits
on the metal steps, gets caught
between two boys fighting.
One spits hard, hits her.
"Sorry," he says, and he means it.
She lowers her head, curls her hands
deep in her pockets, feels
spittle burn cold on her cheek.

Crossing Over

The move to Queens wouldn't have been so bad
if it hadn't meant going over a bridge.
Stiff girders holding the taxi
over water so peaked and so cold.

Then a new world of isolated houses,
fences blocking off lots of mud;
streets emptied, cars full;
the school a bus ride away.

Everyone thought I talked funny.
"What country are you from?"
So many children, so white.
No one ever moved away.

In the evenings I listened
for my mother's steps, for restless
leaves, for the shifting of my own
sheets on the bed.

I could not understand
the silence, so I filled it with stories.
I told myself we'd go back
over that bridge one final time,

back to West Farms. Back
to the building with Granny
one flight up. I didn't even
need to hold the railing.

Back to St. Thomas Aquinas.
Desks with inkwells and deep grooves
where pencils had pushed down hard.
With initials you couldn't erase.

Back to the subways, the tracks
running high as roofs. In the front car
you can feel the train rock, see it balance
even as it tips into turns.

I told myself we'd go back to West Farms.
I told nobody else.

Nights

Feet everywhere, Granny, my sister,
and I sleep in Granny's bed.
July sticks to my pj's.
My tongue tastes salt on my lips.
Radios blare in Spanish
none of us understand.
Fire escapes fill with people,
some dragging pillows, others
shouting to family or friends.
If the shouts become screams
or bottles break into weapons
I cover my head with my pillow,
try not to remember Billy
strutting these streets,
stabbed for fifty cents.

And I don't. Darkness
lulls us. We drift
into its rhythm, wake
to its remnants.

Visiting the Bronx Zoo

On display the lions prowled
restless circles in cages too small.
I remembered the early Christians,
feared becoming an afternoon snack,
held tight to the bar keeping me back.

I moved from African plains
to polar bears yellowed with swimming.
My legs grew into the zoo's green. I learned
to climb its trees, to be "it" in tag games.

Some days I rode a pony or a camel
or took the zoo train, watching leaves
reflected in its awning. I threw bread to ducks
or watched a goat swallow a popcorn bag.

Every Sunday, the same after-Mass afternoon.
Daddy with a ball and mitt, Granny
with a fruit basket, Mommy walking acres
of clipped grass and paved roads.

Our treeless Queens yard measures 20 X 20.
Squirrels and birds never cross the mud.
But local boys shortcut through,
trampling the seedlings, threatening
our plans for a colorful spring.

She Sees an Addict

He's slumped,
a lost man in an abandoned
building. His eyes are marbles,
their glaze impenetrable.
His body's a washrag,
the water all squeezed out.

She knows what he's done,
though some may think she is,
at ten, too young. She's heard
about the needle, how you stab
it deep into your veins. The drug
runs through you until
those who kissed your cheek,
parted your hair, cannot bear
to recognize you.

She clings to the splintering
doorway unable to enter
that space or leave it.

She will remember his stare
fixed as the night,
his body rehearsing death.

How to Walk in West Farms, 1964

1) Understand you are the one who understands. Granny is locked in the streets of fruit carts and milk trucks. Nancy's so young she doesn't even see how children eye her wisps of blond hair.

2) Look straight ahead, but watch the spaces on your sides, the shapes that may be watching you. Listen to the shadows behind you.

3) Be alert, not afraid. These people live here. They just want to buy groceries, catch buses, hang out with friends. They're not criminals. Except some are.

4) Walk fast, with purpose, like you're going on a hot date or a job interview.

5) You won't get lost, but if you do, don't show it. Scan the streets. Pick the busiest one. Walk until you see a street sign, a billboard half ripped out, a church's locked door —something you recognize. If, after ten minutes, you find nothing, find a woman, middle-aged, maybe carrying a shopping bag. Be polite. Use your little girl voice. If the lady speaks English, she'll help.

6) When you get home, Granny won't have the key out, so watch as her hand scrapes around in her purse. Once you're in, check the lock. Check the lock again.

7) Settle in the armchair across from the easy chair, kitty-corner to the window. The same place it's been since you were four. Watch your legs safely dangle.

I Made a Promise

"When you leave you must remember to come back for the others. A circle, understand."
Sandra Cisneros, The House on Mango Street

One more white-skinned family
packing up our Bronx lives

The Castro convertible, easy chair
strapped shut. Easter-egg-colored
Melmac dishes cushioned with pillows.

Just nine years old for just two weeks,
I was too young to understand.
Or too young not to.

"But, Mommy, why can't we stay?"
I knew the feeling of the railing in the hall,
the texture of creviced wood on my feet,

like I knew my mother's hand
stroking back my hair, even as we
looked past each other at the movers.

In the yellow cab to Queens,
I clutched the wrist of my bride doll,
its white gown dripping city slush.

All through the ride I cried, "Good-bye"
to the Bronx home that needed me.
"I'll come back. I promise. I'll come back."

On Tremont Avenue, 1961

Allowances in pocket, we walked to Tremont Avenue.
With fifty cents, I bought a ball.

Felt its perfect roundness, watched it bounce,
and knew sometimes you see what you want and get it.

And that's why hunched-over ladies, paint-splattered men,
permed women pulling toddlers all pushed their way to bargains.

Even as we darted to the sale table or elbowed out
other arms reaching for the same thing, we never felt

our bodies stiffen with fear like they did when we passed
the lots of broken bottles, bent spoons and worn belts,

bare-boned dogs scrounging remnants of remnants.
On Tremont Avenue we were safe and shopping satisfied.

Nothing we bought there lasted long. But we'd go back,
buy another, forget about what was broken or lost.

Old Friends

A head shorter than every other
eight-year-old kid, but that's not
what I notice. It's the swagger

in his John's Bargain Store pants,
the confidence of his plaid shirt
strutting down Daly Avenue.

The third-grade answer to cool.
The in-crowd starts with him.

My visits back are short. I miss
the double Dutch games and trips
to the candy store. Billy's face becomes

a dot in the second-grade class picture.
Till Angela, one of two friends still
in West Farms, leans into the windowsill

in Granny's living room, looks into
the sky speckled with buildings.
Till Angela says, "Billy got stabbed

in the neck. He had fifty cents on him."
I never hear if Billy lives. I never see
Angela again. Her family moves

back to St. Thomas, an island where
her father drives up green hills
to a single wooden house,

its yellow slats crossing the horizon,
where the water is clearer than a mirror.

Safety

I
Mommy told me gangs beat a boy
with baseball bats. Mrs. Sinkowsi's purse
was snatched on her way to the butcher.

Mommy told me we were moving
away from the bad people. I wanted
to tell her: The good people should stay.

But my mouth made only hollow sounds.
Tears washed away my words while her hand
stroked my head and I burrowed into her apron.

II
Our new neighbors peer through windows, scour
my mother's pin curls, my sidewalk games,
my father's lonely waits at the bus stop.

When little Tony throws a shovel of dirt
on my ironed white blouse, I yell.
Seeing his mom, he balls his hands

over his eyes, rubs his tears.
"Fresh girl!" she snaps, not seeing
the smeared top that speaks for me.

From our porch my mom defends me:
hands planted on hips, voice reaching
the entire street.

His mom's laugh hangs in the air
as she marches home,
Tony draped over her shoulder.

Her friends make a gauntlet of stares.
Their anger burns into my summer arms,
cuts through my sweater like December.

But I never know how much they scare me
until years later Tony is arrested: for rape.

I see the glittering switchblade against her neck.
Her protests swallowed. Hair unraveled, tangled.
Heart beating fear, waiting for pain.

Missin' the Bronx Blues

Want to buy some candy
but there's no candy store.
Just lawns of burned blunt grass,
rowed brick homes. What a bore.

Got those missin' the Bronx blues.
Missin' the Bronx blues.

Mom's too scared of drivin'
so we wait for the bus.
Cold cracks my knee-socked legs.
I squeeze my pee; don't cuss.

Got those missin' the Bronx blues.
Missin' the Bronx blues.

Night streets here are nothin'.
Nobody wants to hang.
They talk with curtains drawn.
Their accents all the same.

Got those missin' the Bronx blues.
Missin' the Bronx blues.

At nine Richie was mine.
Gave me a Woolworth's ring.
But when he said "Bronx Spics"
his love didn't mean a thing.

Got those missin' the Bronx blues.
Missin' the Bronx blues.

They say the borough's burning.
They say it's full of crime.
But I know I felt homed there.
I say the Bronx is mine.

Got those missin' the Bronx blues.
Missin' the Bronx blues.
Those missin' the Bronx blues
got me.

Trying to Breathe

For the Girls: Mom Speaks

I'm sorry if I hurt her, but I had enough.
The neighborhood was getting bad. We just wanted
to get the girls out. It wasn't easy.
Even with the VA mortgage, we scraped
through all our savings. What if Mike got sick?

We thought he'd take the bus to work, but that bus
never followed any schedule. He'd be waiting
and waiting, worrying he'd get docked.
And it was a long walk from the last stop to the bridge.
Especially at night. With the roads so dark, I was afraid
he'd get hit. Just like the truck hit my dog when I was a kid.
Broke her neck in an instant. We had to get a car.
The money we saved for an oil heater — so we could stop
shoveling coal and seeing dust coat everything — that's all gone.

Mike had a license, but he'd never had to drive.
So nervous, he put in seat belts he'd read protected you
in an accident. Made me sit in the back seat.
People on their porches looked at us like we were cuckoo.

We did it all for the girls. We could have lived
with the roaches, and the street fights, and
the Negroes moving in. But we wanted the kids to live
in a nice place, in their own house, with their own yard.
Nancy was all smiles and making mud pies outside.
Her first week at the new school she made friends.

Michelle just cried and moped around. She'd sit
at the window and stare at the Whitestone Bridge,
the same bridge where her father takes tolls.
Eight hours a day, car after car, the same hand reaching out.

I didn't know what to do with her. I told her she could
live with Granny for awhile. "No, Mommy, I'll miss you."
Then while cleaning I found one of her poems.
She called the Bronx her Atlantis. I was so fed up.
I turned off the TV she was watching and waved
the paper at her yelling, "That old neighborhood
is no Atlantis. It's a SLUM. No one wants to live there."

Her face sunk like she was stunned, but her eyes
deepened like I said something she already knew.
She went to her room with that poem, stayed there
for a couple of hours. Weeks later she still mopes,
but we never hear any more about the Bronx.

Sometimes when Mike takes me to buy groceries,
I pull the seat belt across my hips, clip in, and remember
walking to the stores while the girls were in school.
Going over the long week's shopping list, I wonder
what my daughter thinks we've missed.

Trying to Breathe

Before his cup of instant coffee,
before brushing his teeth
or turning on the a.m. news

Dad cleared his throat.
Swallowed hard. Coughed hard.
I counted the minutes.

Was it standing in that tollbooth?
Rain   snow   wind
the only elements we worried about.

In Hunts Point, the air is thick
with slaughter. Diesel fumes hang
like eviction notices.

In Soundview trucks, on
pockmarked winter streets, try
to drive garbage out of our lives.

In West Farms   Morrisania   Mott Haven*
a mom urges the cabby "Hurry, God, hurry!"
Listens to her wheezing baby's heartbeats.

In the ER a plastic mask delivers air.
Doctors warn of dust mites   cat dander   roaches.
If only these were the problem.

They prescribe steroids inhalers shots.
If only these were the solution.
Dad spits into the sink as we wait for breakfast.

"Gotta clean out the pipes when you get up."
If only we could dissolve pollution like boiling water
dissolves granules of instant coffee,

transforms it into what Dad cups in his hands.
Lets linger in his throat. Feels its warmth opening his eyes.

Neighborhoods in the Bronx, as is Hunts Point.

Granny Moves to Kingsbridge Road

When those boys threw Granny's brother — seventy-three-years-old and just a little drunk —down the stairs, and he crumpled like a shirt falling off a hanger, Uncle Andy said, "Enough, Mom. You're moving near me. I already got the place. Rent starts next month."

Helping her pack, I stare into barrels and boxes, fold tablecloths, wrap vases, wrap dishes in newspapers till my hands are grayed.

Granny wanders the rooms looking at everything like she sees nothing at all. The handkerchief blotting her eyes does no good. "I cry just like you, dolly, when you moved. Twenty years I lived here."

Safety costs Granny one bedroom and more rent. Her brother, Woyko, takes the couch. My mother shakes her head: "It's still the Bronx."

I hope the neighborhood last longer than their bodies, sagging down Kingsbridge Road, feet finding every step. Unable to absorb the shock of new streets.

Woyko

Everyday he went out, walked a while, drank a few,
came home, slept. But one day he didn't.

The police said people walk off for a reason.
Men don't want to be found. But an old man

barely garbling enough English for groceries,
arguing only in Ukrainian — he didn't want to be lost.

I put on a pretty (but modest) top, dug out my crucifix.
Walked into the Kingsbridge Precinct. Smiled.

"Help me find my old uncle." The officer scribbled notes,
added to the file while Granny drank Woyko's whiskey.

Mom and Dad called every city office in the Yellow Pages.
Always on hold, they always slammed the receiver.

One night my sister got her boyfriend's car.
Without telling Mom and Dad, we drove to West Farms

thinking, maybe, he'd gone to the old neighborhood.
But the old neighborhood was boarded up, padlocked,

mostly burned down. We drove eyeing men
bent over in frayed clothes. Always too young.

Months later the morgue called about a John Doe.
Wandering streets, unable to say his name, Woyko was housed

in a homeless shelter where he wasted away in silence.
Died empty as the buildings our eyes scoured for him.

Granny in the Nursing Home, 1976-1978

Shoulders permanently stooped, women shuffle behind their walkers. On weekends they sit by the windows, hoping suburban sons will stop by. As the sun recedes, they sink further into their chairs and memories. The few men belt their pants high above their waists, trying to hold on.

Uncle Andy sent Granny here. Unemployed, battling throat cancer and whiskey, he's tired of visiting her spoiled food and crusted dishes. "Sign the papers, Mom." She doesn't want to be with people who live their final years meal tray to meal tray. But with Woyko gone, the Kingsbridge apartment, never a home, is a hollow space echoing loss. "Just don't put me in with some 100-year-old woman."

Alice, thin strands of white hair crossing her pink scalp, is 98. She and Granny share a room furnished with two dressers and two twin beds — like two college freshmen. Except neither of them is excited or starting anything.

Granny wears the faded shirtwaists, buckles hardened and cracked, that I remember from as long as I can remember. A super's wife, up at 4:45, checking the furnace, baking bread, feeding her kids. Some ladies here perm their hair, paint their nails. They play Bingo; make paper flowers. Granny walks the halls. I walk with her, keeping her away from the windows. Then I go back to my own life across the river. Back to my plans for graduate school and miles between me and my family.

When she moans softly, the nurses hear one more addition to the cries, mutterings, and pleas of other residents. When her moans get louder they sigh, certain it's arthritis in her knees or back, or a child who died, or the cumulative weight of seventy-eight years.

When she stops making her bed and retracts under her covers for hours, maybe days, a nurse checks. "Anna," the woman in white says to the woman covered in white. Standing at the edge of the bed, she touches Granny's left foot. Touches the toe that, festering and black, falls off.

Granny Refuses the Amputation

"Cut it, leg? I not chicken. No."

First she lost the apartment and everything
that could not clean or clothe her. No room
for memories in the nursing home.

Then she lost her life savings, though
with $5 she tried to open a new account.
Too little.

Then she lost the forty acres she'd tried to till
into a farm. When you can't read you don't know.
Two initials, land gone.

Now they wanted to take the leg that had curled
under her as the ship lurched and wavered
toward America.

The leg that steadied her as she shoveled
coal into the furnace, all the residents
warmed before dawn.

Cut it? A new plastic leg? You don't put on
a leg like a babushka. "If I die, I die. I'll see
my brother and my husband."

Her moans mingled with the rosary, fingers
tracing the smooth roundness of each bead,
feeling crucified Christ's bent knees.

When she could no longer mouth prayers
she waited for her soul to leave her body.
A body aged, diseased, but intact.

Granny's Funeral

After the gangrene ate through her toe and it fell right off …
After the gangrene spread up the leg and she wouldn't
let them amputate …
After the day when I tried to hold her hand and ran,
knowing what I reached for wasn't there …

Her funeral was at St. Mary's Ukrainian Catholic Church
on a street where General Washington, Father
of Our Country, escaped the Hessians.
In a church where they'd never said Mass in Latin.
In a neighborhood where the funeral party had the only cars
that worked. Where the church was one of the few
places still working. If barely.

Outside, the garbage in lots shifted subtly.
Boarded windows locked out the sun. A few people,
lonely in their sparse buildings, watched the whites in black.
Inside, the altar boy swayed incense, chanted
in a language I'd never learned. Short, stoop-shouldered,
thin; he was, maybe, older than my grandmother.

For years I've been away from these streets, this religion.
I enter an alien, documented by mourning.
St. Mary the Protectress, I kiss your sorrow.
The gold background can't minimize how small Jesus is,
curled in your arm. How you can't protect him
from his future of outstretched arms nailed into wood.

Waiting

I stand here with my thumb out waiting
for someone to give me a ride.
I'm wearing my long underwear,
but it's so cold the wind whacks
right through it. My legs can't stop
shaking, and my hands in these rummage-sale
gloves prickle no matter
how much I rub them together.
I keep trying to feel my feet
through the socks and uniform shoes.
I'm a diabetic now, you know?

I had to move out Florence and the girls.
Couldn't let my family stay in a neighborhood
that was turning. I figured we'd move near
the Whitestone Bridge so I'd be close
to work. Thing is the bus near our house,
that Q17, never comes. So after a couple
of weeks of just waiting, sometimes
over an hour, I figured I'd hitch
to the Q20 that runs more often.

Do I look like a murderer or something?
The cars just whiz by like I'm not
even here. I've gotten so cold
I'm ready to walk back to that bridge
and jump. People would notice that.
Yeah, but I wouldn't …

I haven't driven in 15 years —
never needed to. Who'd spend
the money on a car when you have
buses and subways just around the corner?
But it's not like that here.

The fellows I work with tell me
to buy a used car. Go down to the lot,
get one for a couple hundred bucks.
But with all the money we spent
on the down payment, the lawyer,
the moving company. And how much
does it cost to keep a car running?

The dark is settling in.
The headlights glare into my eyes.
The drivers don't look at me.
Their legs never ease off the gas.
Maybe they're afraid. But I think
they just love the moving on and hate
anything that slows them down.

Learning

Peacock Escapes from Bronx Zoo

The other animals, even the other birds,
were locked behind bars, but the peacock
roamed freely among visitors

who admired his feathers, waited
to see them rainbow spread, never
thinking of the thousand eyes watching.

Year after year, the seasons
changed predictably, people of
different races made the same "Ahhs."

One day he looked at the fence
that marked off his home. Saw
it was no higher than the trees

where he'd roost. He'd heard
about the trouble outside and
wanted to see. He flew,

not very surely or well, but
his wings carried him into the sky.
He surveyed all they'd kept from him:

The open hydrants and cracked windows.
The littered lots and dogs with ribs
protruding so it hurt to look at them.

The men clustered on corners,
always waiting. The women slumped
into doorways, marking the days.

One day while watching men bang
dents out of crushed car bodies,
he was captured. His fugitive

status ended. Examined,
declared healthy, he was returned
to his habitat. The staff

worried he'd fly off again.
But with the sights captured behind
those thousand eyes, why try?

Left Behind

First Ricky, then Jim, then the Connollys
next door. Then the Burns who lived
down the hall. Even the blacks and Spanish
who moved here years ago … left.

But the Harpers, they're good Catholics.
Once, Mrs. H. slunk into the confessional,
confessed in almost-whispered words
she was taking The Pill.

Three kids in three years, she couldn't
remember what sleep was. Her husband
couldn't pack enough overtime to fill
those children's mouths.

The priest's voice got gravelly rough
like the screen between them, too thin
for Mrs H, clutching the sweat
in her clasped hands.

"Selfish woman! God has given you
the gift to bring life into the world."
Four more babies followed. The apartment
seemed to shrink to the size

of that confessional. The dollars
coaxed with powdered milk, day-old
bread, refused to stretch far enough
for a home further north.

Her children's freckled skin burned red
in the summer streets. The younger ones
talked ghetto. She tried to slap
standard English into them.

Sometimes Danny got into fights.
Seemed the black boys wanted to see
his white skin crack and bleed.
Or maybe he, always angry, hit first.

Still, the family paid for Catholic school
where they thought their children safe.
But everyone looked at their Irish eyes
and the subway stop where they got off

and saw failure. "White trash," they call it.
Like a blank piece of paper
you crumple and throw away.

Food Stamps Sonnet

This month three days waiting for mail.
Doling out canned soup and buttered crackers.
Adding sugar to opaque black coffee.
Her late-day call to Social Services
brings only ring ring ringing. No one there.
They've gone home to full plates, second helpings.
She hangs up. Dials another number.
The rings persist. Never pause. It's as if
the phone itself is waiting for someone
to soothe it, cradle it. Or like the rings
are her own cries. The cries that snap her boy
from his nap. Bring him running, swallowing
sobs, watching her hurl the receiver
into the wall and smash into the floor.

Roaches

crack out   of cupboards,
dart
    under the stove,
settle into the rust drip
            of the kitchen sink.
Even creep up the creviced
      bedroom wall.

Crush them with shoes
or newspapers   rolled into clubs.
Spray them till you
            cough up fumes.
Turn your cat on their rapid legs.
                They live. They breed black
specks of resistance.

They are harder than the crunch
of their shells. Harder than 3 a.m.
                streets without light. Harder than
the sidewalk
      when you're thrown down,
grocery money
      grabbed from your hand.

But tell that to the people   uptown
in their TV homes with wall-to-wall
cushioning.   Tell that to the people
living   across the water,   watching
children play in grassed lots.

To them the answer   is as clear
as the crossed bones on bug spray:

Roaches live in dirt.   Live with dirt.

Memories of Orchard Beach

We carried coolers, baby oil, toy buckets, and towels
to the number 6 train. Rode to the very end of the line.

A caravan, we walked to the BX 12, the early sun
toasting us as it warmed to late morning.

Halting from stop to stop as the crowds climbed in,
we jolted with the bus on its way to Orchard Beach.

Then we filed out to our chosen parcels of sand.
Spread our blankets like welcome mats,

bottles of soda and *cerveza* securing them
against the welcome breeze.

We breathed the spray of salt air,
took shallow dives into brisk waves.

Our muscles, aching and knotted from lifting
boxes, garbage, children, bills,

loosened like the sand itself, molding
to our bodies, cradling us.

So what if the water was tainted brown?
If the beach was man-made by a man

whose name we spit out like so many
empty hopes scratching our throats?

In the rhythm of the drummers, in closing
our eyes we saw *playas de Borinquen*.

In the rhythm of the tides we felt
Borinquen, la gente de la isla, Nuyorican.

The memory like a wave you try to ride,
hoping it doesn't pull you under.

And if it does, you float in surrender
till another wave pulls you to shore.

Riding a City Bus in July

We read, learning algebra or English,
scribbling notes, sometimes munching lunch.
We underscore thick pages
beyond food stamps and overdue notices.

We nod off. An hour ride is long,
and too little time between jobs or looking for jobs.
Too little time away from bosses wanting or ordering.

We stare out the grimy windows that streak men
waiting on corners, too tired to be restless;
that blur children braving streets for stickball.

We lean back by the open windows, relish
the breeze in a city that drips heat.
But on the street, the hydrant offers the only relief,

passing traffic a substitute for tag games.
Closed eyes are shocked open when the water
rushes into the bus, baptizes us in laughter.

Lehman College, 1970s: The Campus

We schedule classes around cashier jobs, run for the El,
type essays at the kitchen table. But the campus

in various stages and lengths of green
makes us feel like real college students.

Between classes on those teasing spring days
jeans sprawl across the lawn, joints pass hand to hand.

Some of us breathe in daily, let smoke out slowly,
like an unfolding dream. Some test tokes,

feel the firm soil under their butts. Some don't
inhale at all, but just sit in these spaces

where everyone shares and laughs.
Before we return to our classes and our note-taking.

Before marking our calendars for the soc. paper,
the bio. test, the shift change at the supermarket.

Before marking the years, then months, then days
till we graduate. Till our parents cry and snap

photos, and we let out our breaths hoping
the diploma is not the only prize.

Climbing the Steps of Carman Hall

As if this were the Philly Museum she pounds
up steps   steps   steps.
Each time her thighs pull they yank at a picture
she's tried to bundle in the back of her mind:

She's prepping in the library for Brit. Lit. I,
absorbing sun rays between classes.
But she's not a student. She's paid
to teach the books she's reading.

A slight gasp: Do people like her get PhDs?
Dad worked his way to collecting tolls. Mom tended
the kids after 18 years of clerical shifts. Never earning
more than she could pack into a taxi for a move.

Her legs throb arrogance or fear, but the image
of her at a blackboard, chalk pressed firm and steady,
is too clear to ignore. She'll drop the safety
of social work, apply to grad schools, move away.

But she won't tell anyone her choice.
Not parents, or teachers, or furrow-browed friends.
She's too afraid of even one of them laughing,
holding her warm dream in hand, and squishing it.

Learning

My boyfriend Ricky meets me at the subway,
and we get into our fastest, widest New York pace.
Walking through Saturday's rhythms to get to his place.
Hoping his parents go out for groceries,
and we have a couple of hours in his single bed.

He was born in Highbridge, played there,
hated there, knew every bodega, and every guy
who hung out on the hang-out corners.

I don't want to be, but I'm the GIRL FROM QUEENS.
Memorizing the street names and blocks to walk down.

Then we get to his block, see people shift to circle two boys.
They're maybe ten years old. Brown fur collars their denim jackets.
Gang wannabes or more. Throwing down insults.
Then one throws a coke bottle. It shatters,
empty, marking the sidewalk with glass.

Yanking at Ricky's hand,
the only part of him that moves at all,
I say, "Let's go!"
"What!?"
"He threw a bottle. There's gonna be trouble."

Ricky's eyes roll, and he sighs out the thick air.
"He threw it at the other guy's feet.
If he'd been serious, he would've thrown it
at his head, would've cracked his face open."

As we walk away my eyes search the streets.
What I found in that slowed-down walk to Ricky's
I hold decades after letting go of his hand.

Watch how a person makes his mark.

What he is willing to shatter.

What I Didn't Know about Hip Hop

On the number 4, I re-read Ralph's Dear Michelle letter.
He's joining a band. In South Africa. Apartheid.
Mandela. Not even in parentheses.

My rhythm and our life not even in parentheses.
No one notices as I hold the pole gripping
for some future or some vestige of myself.

Sedgwick Avenue's a happenin' place
DJ Kool's transformin' the space
Mixin the break beat, scratchin' the sound
Kool's the coolest rhythm we ever found.

Alone at the New Year's Eve party. Helen's diamond shimmers
against red nail polish. Couples dance the box of the Hustle,
platform shoes stomping out '72. Midnight Helen and Alejando
hug me.
Kiss around me, I'm almost lost in their arms.

They call it break dancin', and I could see
Those gymnastics would break a girl like me.
Head stands and flips right on the concrete
Crowd's formin'. Crowds warmin' to the break beat.

Flexible enough to split my legs flat on the floor, ready to shake
My booty to the beat and shout out lyrics of rock, why wouldn't
I dream of the stage? Ralph gone, I'll never dance with the band.
Never etch my name by gyrating my body.

Hip hop comes out of the Bronx's heat.
Graffiti colors the grayed-down street.
Raps speak out stories never heard.
The limber body. The spoken word.

My own words were pounded out on a manual typewriter.
Scratched out. Whited out. Handed to professors for red scrawls
I couldn't decipher. No guidance. No direction.

Writin' my name in graffiti on the wall.
Check it out. Check it out.
He's not askin' permission.
He's not sittin' home wishin'
He's writin' his name in graffiti on the wall
You might deplore it, but can't ignore it.

Wrong race. Wrong stop on the subway. I clung
to earnest folk blowin' in the wind. To Joyce and Eliot.
Big boy moderns across the Atlantic. Scrawled
Non serviam across my notebooks.

Years later Blondie's "Rapture" makes MTV.
Debra Harry raps on the Man from Mars
eating cars, then bars, even guitars.
So hungry.

The Co-Op City Resident after 9/11

"My cousin worked in the Towers,
and I'm worried. She's not the same.
The job is gone. She hasn't looked
for a new one. She hasn't gone out at all.

Sitting inside in her bunny slippers,
she cries most of the day into the night.
She was always happy in that apartment.
The whole family was happy when they left

West Farms almost twenty years ago,
when she was a niña starting school.
Co-Op City's hallways were lit and Lysol clean.
Parquet floors shone under stocking feet.

No mice or roaches to chase across the room.
The heat, the doors, the windows worked,
and no one lurked on the corners
grabbing purses or knocking men down.

It was so good they got away. But with the attack,
the smoky hallways, so many flights of steps,
some older people pausing too long. Everyone
in her office survived. But so many did not.

Maria sits blank-faced by her window,
staring at other windows and a still sky.
The ears on her slippers flop as her legs rock,
trying to shake out memories.

A Summer Vacation

Blooming hills crossed the TV screen.
Ads for thick forests filled the newspapers
spreading across our couch. We wanted
those pictures to be our pictures.

The farm was a place I'd never seen,
but imagined waves of grain greeting me.
My grandparents imagined working a farm.
The hogs my father had never raised.
The canning a memory from Ukraine.
The soil threaded with rocks.

How long before they realized the city
was in the tips of their fingers?
They couldn't get a grip on tools?
How long before they shuttered
the windows, installed locks,
and left the land to itself?

When our car pulled up to handle-high weeds,
I saw no wheat or corn combing the air.
Just a fading white house, its boxed
structure only hinting at the hollow inside.
No electricity. No running water.

Not even a toilet. Like we were stuck
in a history book picture, still fading. I wanted
the sureness of asphalt streets. The pruned peaks
of the Catskills beckoning us from the networks.

Then we rode past real farms. Rotated crops
carving color wheels in the hills.
Grass chopped to walking length.
Wooden shacks worn frail, so slotted

Learning 59

I could watch the light enter. Shirtless men
or men in sweat-stained T-shirts
sitting on steps in the cooling dusk.
Women with bandanas covering their hair
like Granny with her printed scarves and braids.
Migrant workers, Dad told me, they follow
crops from farm to farm, shack to shack.
No electricity. No running water. No toilet.

No expectations, except hours of bending over
row after rows of crops, unflinching.
I wanted to meet eyes with a man peering
out from under his hat. With a woman
loosening the laces on her shoes. To find
a girl shaking the dust out of her hair.

Through the smudged glass of the car window
I couldn't find their eyes. But I'm telling you I tried.

What He Said

The Master Builder's Cross Bronx Expressway

The squiggly lines converge,
double back, bleed into one another.
I can never follow maps.

But I can follow the clean, slightly curved
artery that cuts right through the Bronx.
Those who can, build, and he built
a highway of concrete progress.

Nothing complicates speed
and pavement. Drivers head
for the George Washington Bridge,
ride into greened lots and pristine blocks
never stalled by the clutter of neighborhoods.

113 streets. 1,500 apartments
in just one mile. On his map,
buildings are small boxes
without people. Easy to cross out.

Those who can't build criticize.
But they had built.
Rooms with paid-for furniture,
measured curtains,
a good school close by.

If he'd lived just a little longer,
and learned to drive …

I can see him sitting
on the Cross Bronx Expressway
traffic halted, cars packed
tight as summer's air,
each exit a broken promise.

The Arson Years, 1970-1980

It costs to heat the pipes. Keep water in the faucets.
Repaint walls chipping lead.

So the landlord stopped. Some left.
Others bundled coats on beds, blasted their ovens, carried
buckets from hydrants, walked up flight after flight.
Only one way to get rid of renters with nowhere to go.

He ripped out copper pipes and lighting fixtures.
Then hired a torch to concoct acid and oxidizers, douse
the walls and floors, ignite. The fire burned right through.
Nothing left, but hundreds of thousands to collect. Again.

In five years an average of three fires a day.
Families slept in jeans and shirts, ready to flee.
The sky, always orange, always alight. People prayed
Dios mio ... Jesus, my Savior ... If I die before I wake.

For some, it was the second, the third burn-out.
They escaped grabbing sweaters, IDs, rosaries.
They covered their mouths, their children's eyes,
as they ran from smoke and screams. People,

many people, dying with arms outstretched
on the bathroom's chipped floor. Survivors
with chopped-off fingertips, leather faces,
hiding their fates in an aunt's locked bedroom.

Our ancient mariners harmed no one.
Yet they wandered, throats singed silent,
backs bent as if still weighted.
If you dared look, their eyes told everything:

Some say the world will end in fire.
We say our world already did.

What He Said

Mortal combat: The Yankees and the Dodgers
batting it out for the World Series.
Across New York the same ritual, people
gather around black and white images,

gulp doubts like swigs of beer.
In a decade with so little to cheer
fans pack the stands, face fall's bluster,
its early dusk, stand up and scream.

The stadium's a world of its own
until the end of the first inning.
Then the news shifts to a five-alarm fire
just blocks away at P.S. 3.

Howard Cosell, who backed Muhammad Ali,
who told us he'd tell it like it is, told us
"There it is, ladies and gentlemen, the Bronx
is burning." Years later we'll remember

the pitch and accuracy of his words.
A book and TV series will carry
the phrase like a banner. Until we learn
Howard never said this.

He said the President just days ago
had toured the street. Firemen in the Bronx
had it tough. And the school was closed.
Nobody was endangered. Strange,

Howard never told us what he really said.
Maybe he wanted credit for that ringing phrase,
or maybe he wanted what we wanted:
Someone say: "The Bronx is burning."

The Father

Carrying a baseball bat through streets
where dying of natural causes was a luxury;
hurling tables and chairs into bonfires,
he showed us what it means to burn.

He was the Father of the Darkened Hallways,
of the Bare Shelf End of the Month. Our savior
in the temple raging against those who care
only for the coins in their hands,
the thieves who ruin what's holy.

He raised his voice to be our voice.
He lifted tables, and we lifted City Hall.
Where others razed, he built.
Fresh brick buildings with windows
that sealed out the street. Security guards
in every entry, locking safety in.

For a few years.

Then the Father rode in his chauffeured
shiny black car. His boss brother roamed
the Village in a robe, mocked our sanity.
The Father took a six-figure salary,
said, "I didn't take a vow of poverty,"
mocked the collar holding his neck.

Now our ceilings have God-sized holes.
Showers pour on neighbors below.
Rapes and beat-downs replace
guards he says he can't afford.
The papers call him "slumlord."
We are calling, shouting at him.

It's true what he says. Without him
Hunts Point would have smoldered
to rubble. We would be bags moving
from shelter to shelter ....
                              I remember
the parties. The break dancing
in swept streets. The dinners we shared,
taken from our ovens like newborns.
And I want to thank him, our Father.

But at the tenants' meeting he stood
flanked by guards, his limo ready
for a quick exit. And I remember
the moneychangers. The shock
that always raises my head
out of my prayer book as Jesus
lashes them out of the temple.
Dashes tables of silver into the dirt.

Presidents Visit Charlotte Street

Carter
Jimmy emerged from the limo
with a handful of other suited men
looking ready for a funeral.

The vacant lots they crossed
gave no resistance or recognition.
Each step amplified the emptiness.

Such a sober man, and he found
the "worst neighborhood in the U.S."
"very sobering." Shock and sincerity

coated his throat. He promised help,
ordered, "See what can be salvaged here."
But he could not save his Oval Office.

In America people just don't sit
as oil supplies are strangled,
embassies are stormed,

Americans taken hostage.
Someone gets tough
or someone gets the boot.

Reagan
Looking relaxed in a tan suit that matched
the sign reading DECAY, he held
the mike, shouted: "Carter broke his word."

The words volley between him and residents
who wonder how their government
could get any more out of the way.

"I can't help you if I'm not elected."

"Hey Reagan, my vote for a job."

George H. W.
The first Bush never came. He was busy
preaching compassionate conservatism
looking for 1,000 points of light, storming
Kuwait. The impoverished borough
slipped back into the map.

Bill Clinton
When Bill arrived he didn't need
to make promises or walk around
rubble.

Fenced ranch houses just big enough
to hug their families safe surrounded
a place called Charlotte Gardens.

Having warmed the crowd with his smile,
he waved good-bye, directed his car
to a Manhattan deli. Pastrami on rye.

So thick it filled his hands
before he got his mouth around it.

Happy Land Fire

Shipwrecked African slaves crawled
out of the wreckage to the shores of St. Vincent.
To new lives and families. Carib wives.

Garifuna. To the British it meant
black and Indian. To the black and Indian
it meant exile in Honduras.

Still black, in freedom still different,
their ancestors struggled to toil less, earn more
than one meal to the next on a plantation.
In *los Estados Unidos* hard work could make
an easy life. How did they come?
Illegally? Legally? Why ask now?

In a New York borough on the cusp of rebirth
They partied in Happy Land. Not enough windows,
locked exits, people packed into dancing and drinking.
Stairways narrow as options. But in a strange country
when *La Ceiba** grants a break from worry for a few hours,
why look for an exit?

Maybe that one ejected man, rejected by his girlfriend,
fired from his job. He was Cubano. He was white.
Does this matter? He was a prisoner who lied
his way onto Mariel. Said he was a drug dealer,
not a deserter. Castro said good riddance.
But with her there was no second chance.

No lie she would believe. And she did not believe
his threat: He'd be back. She did not imagine
anger and a dollar of gas snuffing out over eighty lives.
Some ran for locked doors, hoping for a chance
to kick them open. Others slumped at card tables,

fumes filling their lungs before their minds
understood smoke. Lips never moved to utter prayers.
March 25, 1990. Seventy years after the Triangle Fire
sent immigrant girls leaping to death. Desperate.
Or immigrants still in the last minutes taking
that final leap, hoping for a chance.

The equivalent of Mardi Gras or Carnivale, originating in Honduras.

On Fort Apache, *the Movie*

Scene: Beware the Crazed Hooker
Morning light still gray, the hooker
hobbles in her heels, flying high,
tits falling out of her dress.
The cop in the driver's seat rolls down
his window, tells her to sleep it off.

Who'd expect her shaky hand, chipped
nail polish and all, to pull a gun out of her purse?
Two rookies whacked. They never had the chance
even to put down their coffee, now mixing with blood.

Scene: Murphy and the Girl in Trouble
Railroad flat, nothing like a railroad train
steaming ahead on a track. No, these rooms
so small, windowless, seem to close in
on the cops. Still, they find their way through
worried accented voices to the back room,
even darker. The young girl, fourteen,
heaves and sweats, while Officer Murphy
kneels next to her, weakened by the weight
of saying the obvious: She's having a baby.
No winter coat can hide or stop that now.
He coaxes as she pushes, pushes, screaming.
This child, at least, will be all right.

Scene: Payback
Flames fill the open windows, glass bursts, but
no one dares fight the fire. Fed up with mass arrests,
with a police captain who sees them all as cop killers,
who sees them all as fugitives, they explode.

Roofs are firing zones. Men hurl rotten fruit
at cops. Billy clubs cut the air. Cars topple over

as mobs push and cheer. But one couple
makes out on a roof. Till cops find them.

Maybe because the boy's dark skin glimmers.
Maybe because his biceps bulge. Maybe because
the street screams, but he just wants a hot chick.

With the sky as a witness, two cops lift him up,
drop him off the edge like Ford dropped the city itself.
We wait for the body to hit the ground, wanting an echo.

Scene: Isabel and Murphy
Murphy wants her to meet his three kids,
so she crosses the Concourse smiling.
With her coiffed hair, her trim turtleneck,
loose pants, and sensible shoes, she looks
too staid for her age. Typical young woman
dressing so she doesn't look like a daughter.

Or does she dress for another part?
In ten years could she be the mom
smoothing hair, grabbing small hands
to cross the road? Far from Simpson Street.

Scene: Never Trust
On days off she can't recover
from rushing stretchers down the hall,
from walking the floors all day
and walking a gauntlet just to get home.

So she shoots the (occasional) fix,
delivered right to her hospital door.
But the dealer watches her blue-eyed
boyfriend drive away in his big car,

she may as well be in the window.
"Fuckin slut!" She could lead this cop
straight to his operation, bust it to bits, even
if he made bail. He'd have to fix her good.

Her movements slow like a frame
dragged out, and she knows. Barefoot,
frizzed hair, in her pjs, she moves one foot,
then the other, *just get to the hospital.*

When he sees Isabel motionless
on the table, he grabs her as if ready
to dance or carry her over the threshold.
Moving across the floor, he coaxes,

"Wake up!, Come on, wake up"
Until he feels the weight of death.

Lights On, Talking Back
Something weighs on me,
like the heaviness I feel
when I hear Spanish
and understand
only the shouting.

What about the children
playing ball outside the precinct?

Think about the people sitting
in windows staring past
their twelve-hour shifts

How about the men who cheered
when Murphy out-crazied
a crazed man? Got a knife
without pulling a gun?

And the people marching,
fists lifted pride-high,
wielding nothing but their shouts.
'Cause this is *Nueva York*.
All voices are sirens. But some
sirens scare.

Step out of the frame, look
at the real three men blocking
the shoot, their sweatered shoulders
a wall against the fake working girls

who try to slip on spiked heels,
slip into *el barrio. ¡No pasarán!*
And sisters, keep your feet
flat on the ground.

Blackout

1965
Late afternoon, doing my homework
at Granny's while kapusta boiled.
Pipes sizzled as autumn cooled toward winter.

Suddenly the lights went out.
The radio was silent. But my transistor
told us it was a city-wide blackout.

A complete loss of power
that would stretch through the night.
Neighbors who never spoke

gathered to watch the full moon,
marvel at the specks that were stars.
I, waiting for nervous parents

who couldn't move, watched the candles
drip into plates, impressed my
fingerprints into the wax.

1977
It wasn't fair getting laid off. They had it
in for me. Em tried to offer advice
over burgers and fries. Then everything

dimmed. The owner checked fuses,
but we looked out at blocks of darkness,
questions spilling into the street.

Check on the table, we bolted
for the refuge of Em's Yorkville sublet
where the open windows offered relief

as we snaked a clogged drain.
Just a few
miles north, people so hot, so tired

of seeing what they wanted locked away
broke into stores, grabbed clothes,
carried out TVs, even stole fifty Pontiacs

from a lot, their namesakes
gaining nothing, losing nothing.

2003
People decide
to embrace the darkness.

Subways waver above streets.
Riders fan the air, wait. They're freed.

Below the streets are full.
Music blares, people share

food quickly cooked, watch
young bodies shape the night with dance.

Maybe it's better now. Maybe we're better —
or maybe we have new enemies.

We've learned to mesh together,
shield each other against evil:

Bearded men lurking in caves,
hoarding weapons, training terrorists
to incinerate our towers.

Mural for Amadou Diallo

A wall of blue, the four cops' uniforms
wash in, their triangular white hoods
point to the flag, make us glare at its white.

Though that night they wore street clothes
and watched for a black man, slight, young,
a vicious rapist, thrusting himself
into one woman while her daughter watched.

Most of us didn't know about this man.
His serial sins warranted only small boxes
in the backs of newspapers. But if we'd known,
we'd have wanted him caught. Soon.

None of us knew Amadou Diallo.
Twenty-three years old, from Guinea,
promising his mom, "I'm going to college."
Promising himself he'd be a programmer

soon. He'd trade peddling on 14th Street
for a cubicle and code. These years
of coming home in darkness, waking in darkness,
a gateway to his American life.

The cops didn't see a man looking for take-out.
The cops didn't see a man strolling at night.
The man's dark skin and the street's danger
so etched in their eyes they couldn't see

Diallo at all. They shot shot shot shot shot.
Forty-one times. Hit him nineteen times.
Killed him before he opened his wallet
to prove who he was.

White skulls prop up Lady Liberty,
standing algae green like a sickened child
Her grimace reflects Diallo's
stroke-sloped lips. His bleached-out

red shirt brings our eyes back to the flag
and the words "American Dream"
boldly written in American colors.
This scene was not Diallo's dream.

It is not the dream of the busloads
of tourists, but it is what the cameras
capture, as people stand in front of the mural,
trying to frame themselves.

Trickster

The Nightmares End

I
Once a month. Once a week. The same
sheet-soaking dream. I'm lost in those streets;
all voices have been silenced, and no light,

no neon no stars no bulb shines. I got off at
the wrong stop. I wandered into
the wrong neighborhood, the old neighborhood.

No buses trains cabs come here
Streets of rubble and flames
sharp knives firearms puncturing.

My building an Escher maze, hallways
drenched in urine kerosene blood.
Needles shatter the floor.

Hold tight to the railing, walk one flight up.
The walls darken, collapse in on me.
No one lives here. No one lives.

Like a lover whose arms once soothed me
and now pound merciless blows, the home
I once loved throttles me in my sleep.

II
First glimpses from the fences of the zoo
I still visited, traveling cocooned in express buses.
Sights of construction hats, open windows,
some with flowers or faces in them.

I shifted to subway rides, four swift blocks
under the spring sun. Uniformed children
swung lunch boxes. White haired *señoras*
pay half-price, follow signs for World of Birds.

I watch the seals jump for the promise of fish.
The lions lounge safely on their plains.
Moats and rails keep visitors a continent away.
One day I walked to St. Thomas Aquinas, where

a schoolyard holds the street back. The brick
building still intact, waits for fall classes.
I walked to Tremont Ave. where fast food workers
paused in late afternoon, leaned into their counters.

Before going home I bought a Coke at a bodega.
Inside they looked surprised by my light skin.
And that was it. Except the nightmares stopped.

In the Archives

His blue veins bulging through soft hands
that reach for the stack of folders
I hold out like a gift,
                        the archivist asks,
"Did you find what you were looking for?"

I found blueprints that rolled out
to cover half a table. Pre-Google view
blue and white boxes like X-rays
exposing the skeleton of a neighborhood.

I found shelves of books explaining
how rent control, and migration, and
white flight led to fire and rubble.

I didn't find my house on the drawings.
I didn't find a photo of the candy store,
the synagogue, or the stoop. So I took notes.

In the light taps of keystrokes
I remake Daly Avenue, Alexander's,
the restlessness of Bronx Zoo animals
pacing in concrete cages, watching.

The South Bronx, 2011

The knife-edge edge of poverty
grazed our throats. We waited

for the blade to slit our arteries.
So many of us spun around cycles of need.

Days of hunger, nights of tears.
So many lost to guns, or needles, or flames.

But so many survived.

On Charlotte Street, clean aluminum siding
reflects July's sun. Proud flower beds

dot the trimmed grass. Modest fences
remind us families chose these spaces.

In Melrose a woman pushes a cart,
the laundry still warm, folded and stacked.

Her building's a haven for the homeless,
who understand home the way

the thirsty understand water.
Three girls discarded into foster care

now call her Mom. "I'm saved, now,
I'm saving children."

A cycle we'll keep spinning.

She's Teaching in Suburban Maryland

My dream. My escape from the fumes Dad tried to spit up
all night.

From the pans so thin everything Mom cooked
charred to them.

My escape to a place where I'd talk about books.
And get paid.

A four-hundred-acre oasis, off a highway
and a mall,

this college, once planted in Baltimore, part
of the exodus,

the post-war promise of space and greenery for
(almost) all.

On campus trees shelter. Pruned lawns invite
circles of classes.

The city showcases its harbor, crab cakes, the O's.
Tourists gravitate,

snap photos, tread cobblestone streets. It's not
enough.

Industry choked, population dwindling, the city stumbles.
Some say falls.

Miles of boarded buildings confront people
who look.

So many. So many. Driving downtown, I straddle realities.

I don't want to tell this story again, but the story won't end.

A Personal History of the Bronx River

1961
In the park I slip off my shoes,
sit on the grass with the dandelions,
watch the waterfall cascade
into the river.

I've no idea of its constancy or strength
or how cold the water might feel
in my last autumn here.
But I sit letting it fill me,
like when I sit in Mass listening
to a language I can't understand,
but have learned to revere.

1980
Did we think the river would
digest thousands of tires, stacks
of refrigerators, condoms
from uncountable nights
and adolescent afternoons,
even a wine press, unused,
but rusted right through?
Remnants of discarded lives,
forgotten passions, now sunken.

2010
With the garbage extracted
like so many bad teeth and the water
cleansed, the fish that had died or fled
like everyone else, flip their fins
under our eyes.

Learning to explore the river,
I strap on a life jacket, fold
my legs into the kayak, push off.

The shores are thick with greenery.
Trees arch over the river, protecting it.
The current takes my boat as I twist
gently from the waist, guide
the boat floating downstream.

Beacon, 2010

I
Piles of dirty snow, piles of trash;
the air cold and grim, waiting but not
hoping.

Behind a school
there's a lot marked by a rock
big enough for a two-person tent

where jagged women take
their johns, lie down on the ground.
The sex is no colder

than the hours of days broken
by needle tracks. Children know
to avert their eyes, walk straight

into their classrooms where
teachers unpack their chalk,
unwrap their erasers, strain

against the street and the windows
that rattle in exhaustion
that rattle in impatience, that rattle still.

II
"Beacon in the Bronx," atop a hill.
The school's red brick frame,
white arched doorway promise stability.

Promise a thin sliver of our dream
to families from Guinea, Guatemala,
Puerto Rico, Morningside.

Parents pack thermoses of coffee,
shuttle to second, third jobs for notebooks, pens,
another blouse, so she won't be ashamed.

Parents flank their children, walking them
to school, eyes scanning the tent,
warning hookers, warning users: Stay back.

Some push into CB 6 meetings, sit
through a packed agenda in a packed room,
wait till their hands are recognized.

Protect our children. My ten-year-old
daughter asks why why
don't the women wear clothes?

The next morning the same walk.
Every day the same walk. Until the day
it's just another garbage-pocked lot.

The First Shot

No seven-year-old should control fire,
sterilize needles, or hear her parents' fights
rumbling through the project halls.
Every day Mami cries,

"¡Estás borracho!" But today, worry
punctuates her screams: "Juli, I have
to work, if your hands tremble so
you can't give her the shots, who will?"

Looking down from the chair she's pulled up
to the stove, the girl lights the burner, waits
for the blue ring of fire, places her needle
in the pot, covers it with water.

Stunned at what she knows, Mami guides.
Tells her what vein, how much insulin,
and never, never let air bubbles in the syringe.
Muy peligroso. Like glucose invading her body.

The needle cool enough and filled,
the girl holds out her arm, keeps it steady,
though goose bumps dot her skin.
Then pushes her medicine into her vein.

When Sonia comes down from the chair
her parents are muted and wet-eyed.
She is more frightened than she shows,
and more powerful than she knows.

Jackson Heights, 2014

The number 7 grumbles through 82 Street
People grip the railing for descent.

Little Guyana. Little India. Little Colombia.
Bollywood Music. *La Nueva* Bakery. Islam Trading.
Income Tax. Roxanna Unisex. *Foto y video.*

An honors student studies her neighbors.
With a recording device and serious eyes,
she asks, "How did you get here?"

An arranged marriage to a doctor, who said,
"We are moving to America." My husband
and country, the same choice.

A student visa to study engineering:
A job offer, a green card, citizenship.
All before Muslim names ignited codes.

With my mother who handed coyotes wads
thick as her fist. Weeks   months   moving north
scurrying across borders until in the desert night

we crossed that final border. Fifteen years later
we clean your houses. I dream of diplomas.
Life   liberty   the pursuit of *la migra.*

In Jackson Heights seventy languages ring
through the halls of public schools. Children
latch on to familiar words, shrug away others.

Little Guyana. Little India. Little Colombia.
Little New York. The Statue of Liberty we visit
steadily gripping the railing as we ascend to the crown.

Poetry at the Bronx Museum

Spells are not the eye of newt,
the steaming cauldron

the black cat under the moon's
white light.

La Bruja, asphalt black hair taut
as her verses

scans the sounds of three races.
Takes us

from the Middle Passage to a boot-strapped
island, through

the worn streets of *Nueva York*.
They echo.

A *paisano* raps of Arthur Avenue,
of friends who grew

into other avenues and friends who stayed
watching stores shrink

while they grew claiming, sustaining
what they knew.

In the dimmed light, people shift
in metal seats,

focus to recall scenes they thought
had dissolved,

sigh to hear named what they feared
never was.

Memories made flesh. Made word.
Finally heard.

Elegy for a Building

I'm hoping for holdout.
True, its windows will be smashed,
its hardwood floors wet-rotted.
Graffiti tattoos will mark its war years.
Still, my building might be Ithaca.
I, a slight errant Odysseus, forty years
gone, returning now.

The buildings — yes buildings —
are shorter, newer. The streets,
much quieter, afraid to speak
neighborhood too loud.

As I get closer, my stomach churns
the way it did when I was waiting
for test results. The envelope, finally,
in my hand. In a minute, I'd know.

There's too much sky ahead, on the corner
where my house was. Even a burned-out,
boarded-up shell says, yes, your home was here.
Your family contained the rooms that contained it.
Empty space holds none of my memories.

But the space is a playground, its fence shining
fresh silver paint. Safety mats cover the ground
cushioning children when they fall. Unafraid,
they play. Unaware their neighborhood
has been reborn. Oblivious to me, as I mourn.

Trickster

The way I heard it, so many buildings
in Mr. Jacobo's Crotona were shuttered dark.
To City Hall they were city-sores, failures
to tear down, never rebuild. No one lived there.

But Mr. Jacobo did, and he knew everyone
still in Crotona. And everyone he knew
he begged, "Go into those empty buildings.
Bring some old mattresses, a few pots and pans.
Tell the inspectors that's your home."

More than thirty people pretended, the way
people pretend there's Santa and buy presents.
The buildings got to stay, and buildings saved
by the city became worth saving.

I would have made up stories, would have
helped Mr. Jacobo, and he would have helped me.
But I was trapped in my nine years of life.
Forced to leave the Bronx to others.

ABOUT THE AUTHOR

Michelle M. Tokarczyk was born in the Bronx, New York City, and lived there until she was nine years old, when her family moved to the more suburban Queens. She attended Herbert Lehman College — back in the Bronx — and received her doctorate in English from SUNY Stony Brook. She has been active in the Working-Class Studies Association and is known for her critical work as well as her poetry. Tokarczyk is a professor of English at Goucher College. An avowed city dweller, she divides her time between Baltimore and New York.